A BOOK SERIES: ONE

The Transformative Power
of Symbolism and
Religious Teachings
through the
Lens of Psychology

From the Perspective of Devout Catholics

Cristina Leira and Frankie Lee

ISBN 979-8-89526-763-9 (paperback)
ISBN 979-8-89637-990-4 (hardcover)
ISBN 979-8-89526-764-6 (digital)

Christian Faith Publishing
832 Park Avenue
Meadville, PA 16335
www.christianfaithpublishing.com

Printed in the United States of America

Contents

Foreword

Have you ever wondered why ancient scriptures are filled with mysterious symbols and hidden meanings? Or how our minds can find significance in everyday things, just like puzzle pieces coming together? These questions have intrigued thinkers for centuries, including the renowned psychologist Carl Jung, who believed that everything around us could hold symbolic significance. But there's more to this puzzle than meets the eye.

Join us as we uncover the secrets of how spirituality can enhance our mental and emotional health, bringing a renewed sense of meaning and order to our lives. We will explore how rituals, symbols, and teachings can soothe our fears, inspire kindness, boost mental development, enrich our daily experiences, and even help us navigate the complexities of our thoughts and feelings. Throughout history, people have sought effective ways to cope with life's challenges, especially during times of personal struggle. Recent research from different fields, such as neuroscience, neurobiology, neurolinguistics, and neurotheology, has shed light on the remarkable connection between spirituality, our brains, and our overall well-being. Neuroscience is the overarching field that studies the nervous system from various perspectives, including its structure, function, and impact on behavior. Neurobiology is a subset of biology focusing on the biological mechanisms underlying neural function. Neurolinguistics is a specialized field that investigates the neural processes associated with language and communication. While these fields share common interests in the nervous system, they differ in their scope, focus, and interdisciplinary connections.

Get ready to unlock the potential within your mind and explore the profound connection between your spiritual journey and your mental and emotional health. As we journey together through these pages, you'll discover that the synergy between spirituality and neuroscience holds the key to a deeper understanding of ourselves and the path to greater well-being.

The extraordinary findings of this research are by no means limited to this specific religious framework. In fact, in our next series, we will explore different religious and nonreligious communities and the fascinating findings related to how neuroscience, which aims to unravel the complexities of the brain and how it gives rise to thoughts, emotions, behavior, and consciousness, helps us understand how spiritual practices can enhance our life satisfaction. In this book, we embark on a journey to explore this fascinating intersection of spirituality, neuroscience, psychological well-being, and mental health. We delve into the wisdom of ancient scriptures, the profound insights of modern science, and the incredible stories of individuals who have discovered the transformative power of their beliefs and practices. We explore how spirituality provides a personal connection with the transcendent, the sacred, or the divine. In the first book of a six-book series, we will explore a specific organized and structured system of beliefs, practices, rituals, and values centered around a particular set of doctrines and teachings. It is important to mention that we will refer to spirituality rather than religion. However, we will focus on the findings on religious symbols and teachings of the Catholic faith in our first book, followed by the perspective of our subconscious in connection with the modern advancements in artificial intelligence and machine learning on faith in book 2.

Words from the Authors

Dr. Cristina Leira and I come from very different worlds. She is a loving, giving, accomplished, high-achieving, and intelligent individual for whom I have the utmost respect and trust. She was born and raised Catholic. Meanwhile, I proclaim to be religionless. I grew up in a household where my father was an atheist and my mother was a devout Buddhist. As a result, I learned to understand both views and respect the beliefs of others, whatever they might be. I have genuinely believed throughout my life, and I will continue to believe that I need no religion or higher power to guide my path. I trust myself to do no wrong to others, have compassion, and lend a hand where and when I can. I feel utterly and most naturally to be religionless.

—Dr. Lee

Dr. Frankie Lee is one of the most compassionate, generous, brilliant, and successful people whom I also hold in the highest regard and trust. Years of working together throughout the most prolonged hours of the seemingly never-ending iterative process of writing my PhD thesis, Dr. Lee, as the dissertation chair, provided evidence of my deepest beliefs about the intrinsic good nature of human beings regardless of our religious or nonreligious creeds and practices. It may not come as a surprise that, being from a Latin American country, I was raised Catholic since, as per survey data in 2020, 57 percent of the Latin American population is Catholic. However, contrary to expectations, my parents were not practicing or devout religious people. So how could I be born and raised Catholic? Simply put, I was baptized Catholic as a newborn and later attended a Catholic high school. However, from my early years until I was twelve, my daily life did not include attending Mass, confession, or any other Catholic sacraments. My parents chose my secondary school because of its unprecedented educational excellence. That said, I grew up witnessing the power of prayer, faith, and a disciplined ritualistic mind, especially in times of adversity.

To expand on how the first book in this series was conceived, it resulted from informal conversations in our weekly Sunday Zoom meetings that included brainstorming on how to keep collaborating in research. Even though we do not share the same religious backgrounds, the more we worked together, the more we found shared life values and principles that transcend religious affiliations, such as the intrinsic human need to be loved, belong, and survive with ease and grace despite life's adversities. With understanding and conviction of our upbringing, doctrine, beliefs, naturalistic disposition, and respect for each other, we collaborated on this book series because of our very different upbringings, life paths, experiences, and viewpoints.

We started curious about why we differed but agreed with many views. We discussed many topics and ultimately ended up on the subject of religion in America. We were curious about the continuum of contentious faiths in the US, even though the Constitution's First Amendment guarantees that every person has the freedom to exercise his/her/their beliefs. We started with a common theme, which became the topic and focal point of our book series, where we focused on different religions and the principles, histories, and traditions of ordinary people's beliefs and religious practices, such as religious symbols and teachings. We also wanted to focus on modern advancements in knowledge and technology, such as artificial intelligence (AI) and machine learning. We wanted to see how today's world operates, deciphering information through collectively shared information and machine learning through AI, and how the technologically advanced society is impacting the knowledge, perspective, and beliefs of multigenerations, such as on the topic of spirituality.

Modern technological advancement gives rise to thoughts, emotions, behavior, and consciousness to help us understand how spiritual practices have changed.

AI presents a multifaceted puzzle for religious communities. While some embrace its potential to enrich spiritual life through AI-driven prayer or guidance, others grapple with its implications for the divine. Questions arise around AI sentience and its potential influence on the human soul or a higher power. Further concerns lie in potential biases within AI applications, raising anxieties about inclusivity within religious practices. Ultimately, the impact of AI on religious perspectives hinges on individual interpretations and how communities choose to navigate this ever-evolving landscape.

—Dr. Leira

Background

Do you believe your mental and physical gifts and talents are given, external, or bestowed upon you? Do you think a power greater than you—call it a deity—provided you with your faculties, aptitudes, strengths, and the like, unrelated to your efforts or merits? Or do you believe you earned power through your actions, efforts, and personal development? For example, were your wisdom, knowledge, compassion, and spiritual growth cultivated through a relentless quest of self-awareness, practice, and inner work, leading to the development of virtues through conscious effort and personal transformation? This topic has fascinated many authors and spiritual teachers, such as Eckhart Tolle, Deepak Chopra, Wayne Dyer, Don Miguel Ruiz, Joseph Campbell, and Thich Nhat Hanh, among many others. Furthermore, some notable neuroscientists and researchers, such as Richard Davidson, Daniel Goleman, Matthew Lieberman, Antonio Damasio, and Carol Dweck, contributed to understanding power, self-identity, and personal growth from a neurological and psychological perspective.

Numerous studies have explored the impact of religious and spiritual beliefs and practices on human cognition, behavior, and well-being. Faith-based practices and religious teachings profoundly affect cognitive and behavioral functions. However, before going any further, we will maintain clear and consistent definitions for specific terms to avoid confusion. The essence of language is captured in a thought-provoking quote often attributed to George Bernard Shaw: "Britain and America are two nations divided by a common language." This statement underscores the profound idea that even when we use identical words, their meanings can diverge significantly due to cultural nuances.

So what about science, psychology, spirituality, religion, neuroscience, neurotheology, and even AI for the sake of our book? We define science as a systematic and methodical approach to acquiring knowledge and understanding the natural world. It involves empirical observation, experimentation, and the formulation of testable hypotheses to uncover facts, patterns, and laws governing reality's physical, biological, and social aspects. Science aims to provide evidence-based explanations for natural phenomena and relies on principles of objectivity, repeatability, and peer review to ensure the validity and reliability of its findings. Psychology entails the scientific study of the mind and behavior. Its immense scope crosses the boundaries between the natural and social sciences.

Furthermore, spirituality entails a deeply personal and often transcendent aspect of human experience that involves a search for meaning, purpose, and connection to something greater than oneself. It encompasses beliefs, practices, and experiences related to the nonmaterial or metaphysical realm, including concepts like the soul, the divine, and the sacred. Spirituality can take many forms and expressions through religion, meditation, prayer, mindfulness, and other practices. It often involves questions about the nature of existence, mortality, and the pursuit of inner peace and enlightenment. How about neuroscience? In our forward section, we defined neuroscience as the scientific study of the nervous system, including the brain, spinal cord, and peripheral nervous systems. It encompasses a multidisciplinary approach that combines biology, psychology, physics, and chemistry to understand the nervous system's structure, function, development, and disorders. Neuroscience aims to unravel the complexities of the brain and how it gives rise to thoughts, emotions, behavior, and consciousness. It involves neuroimaging, electrophysiology, and molecular biology to explore the mechanisms underlying neurological and psychiatric conditions and normal brain function.

Neuroscience advances our understanding of cognition, emotions, perception, and various aspects of human experience. As for religion, we believe that it primarily centers on organized belief systems, rituals, and communities, often with a theological framework. Religion is concerned mainly with faith, morality, and meaning. In contrast, neurotheology aims to explore the neural mechanisms underlying religious and spiritual phenomena without making theological or philosophical claims. Finally, for the sake of our book, artificial intelligence (AI) refers to the simulation of human intelligence in machines that are programmed to think and learn like humans. AI can include reasoning, learning from experience, understanding natural language, recognizing patterns, and making decisions. AI can be applied in various fields, including robotics, natural language processing, computer vision, and machine learning.

Now let's resume our journey to the transformative power of symbolism and religious teachings through the lens of psychology, from the perspective of devout religious individuals.

Extant research shows extensive evidence that faith-based teachings, rituals, and symbols can promote psychological well-being and restore a sense of meaning and order to help individuals cope when experiencing adversity. We embarked on a long journey of extensive literature review in our quest to understand the power of symbolism and religious teaching through the lens of neuroscience and psychology. We found that within the last few decades, a significant body of evidence demonstrates the positive effects of spiritual practices and beliefs on the faithful's cognitive processes by averting their fear of uncertainty.

Numerous research studies have focused on the implications of religious symbolism and religious teachings on individuals' mental and behavioral functions. The interpretation of religious symbols affects individuals' psychological and social functioning.[1] Other studies, such as Chappell et al. (2020)[2] and Dentale et al. (2018),[3] examined the effects of religious symbols and religious practice on cognition and neurobiology linked to religious behaviors that promote the forging of social bonds. Additional research focused on the

---

[1]   Kovačević, Malenica, and Kardum, "Symbolic Interactions," 30.
[2]   Chappell, Tomcho, and Foels, "Psychology of Religion," 241–246.
[3]   Dentale et al., "Only Believers," 185–194.

influence of religiosity at varying analytical levels on the cognitive health of devout individuals,[4] their physical health, and the relationship between religiosity and self-perceived well-being.[5] Furthermore, current research expands on how the use of religious rituals, symbols, and teachings helps to soothe an individual's fears and anxieties,[6] thus forging prosocial behaviors, boosting mental development, enhancing the quality of their daily lives, and alleviating feelings of cognitive dissonance. These findings constitute an emerging research trend in religious sociology.

Extant literature has well-documented mentions of religious symbols and teachings related to faith that help the mind of the faithful focus on a single element and reduce restlessness. Everything can potentially assume symbolic meaning.[7] Sacred scriptures are filled with symbolic imagery: "The Lord is my rock, fortress, and deliverer; my God, my rock, in whom I take refuge; my shield and the horn of my salvation, my stronghold."[8] It is also known that religious practitioners treasure and preserve their religious symbols to cope and find solace and courage in times of adversity. Commitments to a religious identity can positively predict the self-perceived well-being of an individual. For example, religious beliefs implicit in the Catholic faith can provide a sense of meaning, purpose, and belonging during difficult life circumstances by soothing their fears and concerns. The ritualistic nature of the worship service, with its embedded symbolism, offers a transformative experience to the faithful. More recent studies emphasize the importance of teaching the multisensory dimensions of religious practices, which could generate cognitive alternatives to empirical reality and increase faith learning by positively influencing the faithful's spiritual life.

Based on previous literature, religious beliefs implicit in the Catholic faith of devout individuals hold a strong sense of meaning and purpose and thus often help the devout Catholics lessen their

---

[4]   Stroope and Baker, "Whose Moral," 185–199.

[5]   Carlson et al., "You Shall Go."

[6]   Imperatori et al., "Neuro-Physiological," 728.

[7]   Jung et al., "Man and His Symbols."

[8]   Ps. 18:2 KJV

fears and anxieties, forging social bonds under challenging circumstances. To better understand the effects of religious symbolism, we investigate how devout Catholics use religious symbols and religious teachings to cope with personal challenges. We aim to provide context and understanding of the neurobiological and psychological effects driven by the cognitive and behavioral effects of multimodal and dynamic religious practices and teachings on the faithful. We anticipate that individual responses vary according to maladaptive or adaptive coping strategies. Hence, since religious coping is multimodal and dynamic, it may help enhance the use of resources to cope with personal challenges. We also hope to further shed light on broader social issues, as previous literature has found that religious teachings and the sensory perceptions of religious symbols may generate a sense of social belonging and prosocial engagement. Thus, our study examined the role of religiosity in individuals' self-perceived well-being, which directly impacts their psychosocial, life satisfaction, and health-related outcomes throughout their lifespan. From a knowledge standpoint, our findings were based on empirical research methods that further contribute to the fields of psychology and neuroscience and thus advance scientific knowledge. From a practical and societal standpoint, we aimed to share with the general public the transformative power of religious symbolism learnings and practices from multiple perspectives, such as an increased internal sense of self-worth and a social sense of achieving a better understanding of the societal need to understand better the behavioral and cognitive implications of religious practice and teachings. Ultimately, we hope our findings will empower individuals to constructively assess self-worth and attain a sense of belonging, exerting a beneficial effect by reducing cognitive dissonance. Finally, our study contributed to the body of literature, covering a series of empirical studies exploring the impact of religiosity on individual well-being.

Historical Context and Literature Review

Symbols exist in every aspect of religion. In the context of our discussions within our study, spirituality refers to nonreligion-based practices and beliefs for those who search for meaning and purpose in life, try to make sense of their inner dimension, and do not believe in a higher power. Symbolism embodies sense-making, forms, or linguistic metaphors that convey meaning across shared social worlds. Religious teachings promote interfaith dialogue to understand the diversity of beliefs in different cultures, leading to social cohesion. Symbology and, specifically, religious symbols and religious teachings play critical roles in curving the mind of individuals to a single focus and pacifying its restless nature.[9] The religious faithful affirm greater life satisfaction during times of personal challenges. In the minds of practicing devout Catholics, religion is necessary for the evolution of knowledge and humanity. Religions emerged when intelligent, highly societal beings evolved mental capability for symbolic reasoning and cultural transmission, resonating at a social level. The multidimensional constructs of life, worldviews, symbology, and religious teachings offer individuals a psychological basis for perceiving and comprehending themselves and their social context. Spiritual practice is necessary to stabilize reality, generate confidence, and cancel fear (of cognitive origin) when facing the unknown. Similarly, religiosity may restore normalcy, order, structure, and meaning, particularly in challenging times.

Over the past five years, newer studies have focused on how religion has influenced individuals' mental and physical well-being, eas-

---

[9]   Ps. 18:2; 1 Tim. 3:16–17 (King James Bible [KJV]).

ing fears and anxieties, helping them cope with adversity, and forging social bonds. The scientific community has clinically observed, tested, and correlated wide-ranging effects on mental well-being to religious practices and teachings. These additional findings implicitly impacted the worldview of neuroscience and medicine, leading to new questions on mind-body effects. Research such as[10] this recommends an increased focus on neuro-physiological factors associated with religiosity. Other studies have explored other religiosity elements through intelligent interpretation of symbols and recommended additional exploration of symbolism and religious teachings. The focus on specific religious symbols, such as using the Rosary and other religious symbols and rituals to cope with hardship, has also risen.

Further research explores religiously significant teachings that include emotions and spiritual experiences. Religious thinking and behaviors can help forestall individuals' fear of uncertainty by positively affecting their basic cognitive processes crucial in navigating their social lives. These findings constitute an emerging research trend in religious sociology. Sociocultural teaching and learning are imperative to the mental development of learners, especially those of the Catholic faith. The unique ability of individuals to employ language and symbols to communicate a sense of unity and the coherence of sensory experiences is reached and established by how individuals interact with one another through shared symbols. Society's conceptualization or concept formation depends on the presence of symbols whose meanings are socially applied. Thoughts, self-concept, and interaction with an individual's community are typically created through symbolic interaction. Individuals fostered the development of the religious or spiritual self, irrespective of religious affiliation and practice. Therefore, people could essentially experience the personal aspect of religion or spirituality before it becomes a social phenomenon.

Consequently, individuals assign symbolic meaning to their social interactions. The individual's mind gets, processes, and inte-

---

[10] Imperatori et al., "Neuro-Physiological," 728.

grates social information, then imbues it with personal meaning. Moreover, the mind and self are intrinsically related and allow individuals to negotiate reality through symbol manipulation employing complex mental processes. Ultimately, the functions individuals attach to a particular object, image, or symbol make it meaningful. This meaning is based on what the individual believes rather than what is objectively true. Therefore, humans are best understood in a practical and interactive relation to their immediate environment.

Additionally, an individual's spiritual beliefs and values are behaviors within the context in which they occur. Individuals are shaped by interpretation, understanding, bias, and social processes of learning and transmitting information about the world. This information comes in various forms, including language and symbols, and provides the means for individuals to negotiate meaning. We must remember that beliefs and practices are not sacred unless people interpret them as sacred and create special meaning and significance. Religious activities like ceremonies, symbols, rituals, and teachings demonstrate the importance of social and cultural interactions, especially during events like Masses, Bible study groups, and other spiritual and cultural gatherings.

Religious values play an important role in social and cultural (socio-cultural) functions, assigning meaning to symbols that can, in turn, create a belief system that might affect behaviors and, thus, impact the social and psychological performance of individuals. Indeed, people change and adapt the meaning of the symbols they use in action and interaction based on interpretation. Since religious symbols and religious teachings vary per religion or spiritual practice, we decided to focus on using religious symbology and the sacred teachings of devout Catholics.

Use of Religious Symbols and Religious Teachings

Religion or spiritual practice influences our global view and beliefs about the self and the world upon which we build meaning systems to guide us through everyday life. Faith and beliefs produce an optimistic worldview that promotes sociocultural obligations and, thus, reduces isolation and loneliness. Turning our attention inward through faith or spiritual practice, we experience bodily sensations and the production of an embodiment of emotions while living a somatic inversion, where aspects of our physical existence or bodily sensations typically in the background of our awareness become the central focus of our conscious experience. In other words, we suddenly become very aware of our bodily sensations or physical presence, which we usually take for granted or do not consciously notice in our everyday actions and perceptions. These experiences bring these usually subtle or unnoticed aspects of our physical being to the forefront of our awareness. This process deepens our spirituality or faith, rendering it more palpable and real. This experience creates a feeling of factuality and belief grounded in our religious experience. Since the first written verse, the sacred scriptures have included symbolic imagery of faith. Religious symbols have significant influences, positive or negative, on emotional valence based on intelligent interpretation. Prayers for supplication, intercession, or gratitude are all expressions of religious symbolism or ritualistic form. Therefore, symbolism and spiritual teaching could help the faithful manage crises and illnesses.

Research continues to demonstrate the pedagogical effects that symbolic religious, cultural, and social contexts exert on individuals. Symbolism exists because of intelligent interpretation and is, therefore, individualistic. Anything can be assumed to have symbolic significance. Even when symbolism cannot be rationally explained, it could still help individuals cope with adversity when it is most needed. Recent studies on Catholic instruction, history, and philosophy, such as adult religious education (ARE), rite of Christian initiation of adult (RCIA), and Bible studies, concluded that there was a need to increase catechism and religious education that include sociocultural elements of teaching and learning in individuals' mental development. There is a need for further study to understand the implications of the use of religious symbols and religious teachings to help us cope in times of adversity.

Devout Catholics

From the perspective of devout Catholics, the Catholic faith enhances life satisfaction and psychological well-being. Religious practice mobilizes individuals in different ways by shaping and reshaping the self and the community worldview, strengthening how we perceive God as a "higher being" and how we interpret sacred scriptures. We establish religious norms as necessary standards in life and act accordingly to create stability. In our discussion, it is essential to know that the devout Catholic population is 73.2M, or 22 percent of the US population,[11] and represents 34 percent of the US Christian population (Parishes and the Catholics Population section)[12] in one way or another that applies religious norms. Around 17.3 percent, or 12.7M devout Catholics, attend Mass every week. At least once a month, about 36.6 percent, or 26.8M, attend Mass, and 71.9 percent, or 52.6M, pray at least once a week (Sacraments and Rites section).[13] There are various reasons why devout Catholics attend Mass, pray, and faithfully respect religious norms and traditions.

Liturgical reverence is the foundation of Catholics' identity, tied firmly to their formal worship of God, known as the liturgy. This worship is based on principles like *opus Dei* (God's work), *lex orandi* (prayer), *lex credenda* (belief), *lex vivendi* (life and conduct), and *lex (con) vivendi* (education and training).[14] These principles guide their religious practices and traditions. Preserving Catholicism is achieved by adhering to traditional religious beliefs and practices that reinforce Catholic identity. The ceremonial and symbolic practices activated individuals' spirituality in the search for the sacred. Research has shown positive correlations between devout Catholics and self-efficacy, connecting the capacity to act effectively during the adversity associated with religious practices, rituals, and teachings.

---

[11] Chepkemoi, "US States."

[12] Center for Applied Research in the Apostolate, "Frequently Requested Church Statistics."

[13] Ibid.

[14] Plaatjies-van Huffel, "Rethinking the Reciprocity."

While some individuals tend to become less religious as society modernizes, Hispanic Catholic congregations are among the most proliferating segments of organized religion. Nevertheless, religious commitment requires effort and time. Some spiritual practices have reached a relatively low level in recent years due to factors like the COVID-19 pandemic and overall self-ascribed busier lifestyles and social activities. The adaption of the evolving modern Catholic faith defined the *creative Catholics* as those who only adhered to some religious beliefs and practices, the *orthodox Catholics* as those who fully endorsed all Catholic traditions, and the *cultural Catholics* as those who only practiced certain rituals occasionally but did not believe much in its teachings. We were intrigued by this secular era that defined modern Catholicism and embarked on the journey to investigate how self-ascribed devout Catholics practiced their faith. We focused our study on raising awareness of the significance of effective religious communication. We dwelled on the relevance of religious teachings supporting individuals' belief systems, spiritual interpretation, and the public's understanding of religiosity. We sought to understand what prominent religious symbols and teachings were still relevant in this secular era.

Religious Symbols and Religious Teachings

Religious Symbols

Throughout history, devout Catholics have used religious symbols, rituals, and teachings to cope with everyday life activities, such as praying for better health and well-being, and to help them build resilience in times of adversity. Research has shown that devout individuals who practice religious rituals see reduced mental and physical risks, faster recovery times for various disorders, greater longevity, and better ways to cope with personal challenges. The symbolism of religious rituals and teachings helped coalesce individuals across cultures, languages, time, and space through cognitive, behavioral, affective, and developmental factors. Symbolism, for each individual, can be explained using linguistic and nonlinguistic forms, which correspond with individualistic interpretations and meanings. Religious rituals denote the symbolic interpretation of an experience that positively influences a sense of order, community engagement, and the transformation of thinking. Rituals embody actions with a deep foundation within our bodies and senses. The biological experiences include formality, sequencing, patterning, and repetition to promote positive psychological and social changes. A ritual is meaningful when the experience is close enough to have emotions and distant enough to have a symbolic interpretation of the ritualistic experience. As a result, rituals allow the individual to relive or actively act on one's life experiences.

Emotional charges are also associated with using and interpreting sacred symbols; however, we are barely scratching the surface of understanding symbolic behavior in human evolution. What we learned, which is indisputable, is that religious symbols introduced a new level of cognition and social organization in human development. Symbols are cultural signs, and a practical aspect of the individual's experiences is used in religious rituals to promote well-being, meanings, and the integration of society. During hardship, individuals coping with adversity require mental and behavioral controls to curtail and endure illness, stress, or conflict. Using religious symbols and teachings creates a symbolic and meaningful action to serve as a resource for coping with personal challenges. To exemplify, worship service and its liturgy as an ensemble of signs and actions is a symbolic realization of meaningfulness and reconciliation that ritual actions lead to transformation by learning to cope in times of adversity.

Devout individuals exercise cognitive and intelligent interpretation during worship services, liturgical acts, and religious teachings. This basic form of brain function is a process in which we make sense of situations and experiences that give meaning to the liturgy that impacts our daily lives when affected by misfortune or disease. Among the findings in research, the general public has shown more interest in experiencing the mystical side and the symbolic and ceremonial aspects of liturgy in multisensory worship, as demonstrated by the popularity and following of spiritual and fantasy-based entertainment today in formats such as movies, theatric performances, books, and other literature. Interpretation and enjoyment of symbolic rituals require seeing, hearing, tasting, smelling, touching, and experiencing the meaning of symbols and sacraments, which enhance the quality of individuals' daily lives. Therefore, we looked at how devout Catholics use multisensory religious symbols and religious teachings to cope with personal challenges as our focus to understand the overall impacts on psychological and physiological well-being. We limited our focus to thirteen common traditional Catholic symbols and three specific religious teachings.

In our study, we examined the historical context and uses of thirteen common conventional symbols, which include bells, the church as a worship site, the crucifix, the holy water, iconography, incense, oil anointment, the reception of Communion, the Rosary, sacred scriptures, sacred music, penance, confession, or reconciliation, and vigil candles.

Soundscapes represent the perception of an acoustic environment in a contextual setting, which improved mood, subjective well-being, and life satisfaction when religious individuals were exposed to soundscapes associated with places of worship, such as bell ringing. The ringing of bells from a church tower reminisces about the sound of joy, a reminder of God's presence and blessings. Bells ringing at the church bring people together physically to pray and emotionally connect through shared identity and habits by producing metonymic associations with their traditions and values. For the devout individual, the valence of the bell ringing in the church conveys comfort beyond its call for prayer since it represents the actual embodiment of the voice of God. Symbols constitute the basic building blocks of rituals. They are external sources of information that allow individuals to make sense of and organize the physical and social world.

The Catholic Church, as a worship site for the devout, the "house of God," is a sacred space for self-reflection, prayers, community building, and connection. The church, then, represents a dominant physical religious symbol that evokes strong emotional reactions.

The sacramental cross reminds the faithful of Christ's love, sacrifice, and resurrection and helps them cope with personal challenges. It is a polysemous entity bearing multiple meanings, such as a symbol of the Christian faith, an assertion of Christ's crucifixion, and a healing object for the bearer or supplicant. The cross is a mnemotechnical artifact that helps the devout remember Jesus inside and outside the church, functioning as daily protection to ward off evil and as a reminder of the absolution of sins brought about by Christ's crucifixion.

As for holy water, all life on earth depends on water to survive—the source of life. In religions, water signifies the devout Catholics' birth into the divine, welling them up to eternal life through the Holy Spirit's action in the sacrament of baptism. The Old Testament alludes to its essential qualities to bestow life on earth, cleanse, wash, heal, purify, and show kindness, humility, and hospitality when offered to others. Yet the New Testament indicates that holy water can wash away sins during the sacrament of baptism.

Iconography, or icons, are symbolic representations of the transcendent that enable the faithful to sense the spiritual and mystical reality of God's presence. Iconography symbols are mainly about prayer, embody tradition, and are part of a living culture adapting to changing times, as witnessed by the various materials and modes of production throughout the ages, such as stained glass, statues, and holy cards. There are four major categories of iconographic representations: (a) Christ, especially portraying sacraments such as the Eucharist and baptism; (b) the Virgin Mary, Christ's birth, passion, and crucifixion; (c) universally veneered or geographically local saints; and (d) angels.[15]

---

[15] Mahić, "Two Home Stoups," 137–156.

Images possess some features of personhood, even though they lack the sentience and intentionality humans have, which invite the viewer to experience spiritual comfort and strength in times of adversity. Throughout the ages, for the faithful, the sweet-smelling kingdom of heaven was in direct opposition to the stinking ubiquity of decay and hell. In the early days, the believers perceived pleasant aromas as the reflections of the divine or paradise, and a whiff of myrrh was enough to summon up thoughts of Christ's suffering body. During the baptismal ritual, the priest touched the infant's nose. He uttered the words *in odorem suavitatis* (to a sweet and pleasant smell) to expel the stench of sin. In the house of God, clergy would employ incense up to seven times during a solemn Mass to perform the symbolic rite of the cleansing act. Incense has formed part of many religious events commemorating the change in spiritual status, including the consecration of new churches, altars, burials, blessings of holy anointing oils, and weddings.

Oil has been used throughout the ages for cooking, baking, embellishing the skin, honoring guests, lighting the lamps in homes and temples, and healing; thus, oil is referred to as the *oil of gladness*.[16] For the devout Catholic, Jesus as Christ holds a threefold office: as a priest, a prophet, and a king;[17] hence, as the savior of Israel and being the anointed one, he received the full anointing of the Holy Spirit as king,[18] prophet,[19] and priest.[20] The first mention of the anointing of believers appeared after the Second Vatican Council, where the threefold office of Christ was equated with the ministry of the church and the faithful. Following the *Catechism of the Catholic Church*,[21] the threefold office is now understood as *sensus fide fidelium* (sense of faith on the part of the faithful). This statement means

---

[16] Ps. 45:8; Heb. 1:9 (KJV).

[17] Libreria Editrice Vaticana, *Catechism of the Catholic Church*.

[18] Luke 1:33 KJV.

[19] Luke 4:18 KJV.

[20] Heb. 7:17 KJV.

[21] Catholic Church, *Catechism of the Catholic Church*.

that every believer, based on the faith of the Lord Jesus Christ and the anointing through the Holy Spirit, whether ordained or laity, participates in the threefold office. Ultimately, the sacramental objects, such as blessed oil, perceptible by touch, substantial, and concrete, mediate the religious power for the faithful, especially during times of personal challenges.

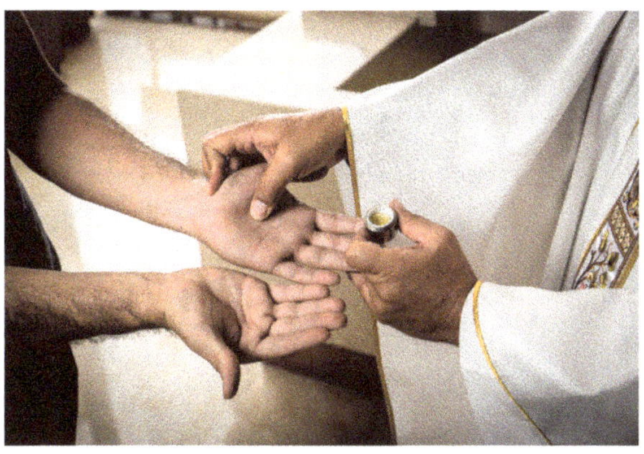

The reception of Holy Communion is the most significant example of embodied spiritual experience within Catholicism. When devout Catholics gather to celebrate Holy Communion, they embark on multisensory worship ritual behaviors that involve interacting with various symbols. It is paramount that the faithful feel a sense of connection between celebrating the Holy Communion and the signification of its meaning, which is receiving Christ himself. The Holy Communion invites cognitive processes that offer the opportunity for vivid remembrance and recognition that will help the devout scrutinize their daily lives with a renewed perspective of the past by having been saved by faith in the resurrection of Christ. The experience of Holy Communion is a wholesome cognitive process, and the faithful must be eager to learn how to be, live, and embrace the affective dimensions of cognition.

Celebrating sacraments aims to lead to practical wisdom, discernment, and sound judgment, or phronesis. Another type of ritualized communication that invites the use of religious symbols occurs during the meditative prayer form of the Rosary. The Cistercian Abbot Stephen of Sally introduced the Rosary in the thirteenth century, and the Carthusian monk Dominic of Prussia modified it. At the same time, Alanus de Rupe simplified it in the fifteenth century. The current version has fifteen mysteries, or statements, grouped into four classical recalling events in the life of Jesus and Mary, prayed on specific weekdays and seasons: the joyful mysteries (remembering the incarnation of God in Jesus) prayed on Mondays and Saturdays; the sorrowful mysteries (related to the passion of Jesus) prayed on Tuesdays and Fridays; the glorious mysteries (about Jesus's resurrection) prayed on Wednesdays and Sundays; and the luminous mysteries (recalling the significant moments of Jesus's public life) prayed on Thursdays. Each mystery has five decades (ten Hail Marys, one Our Father, and one Glory Be prayer). The meaning of the Rosary beads is to keep the faithful from falling asleep or losing count as they pray.

Prayer is crucial to any religious identity. The Rosary is an intercessory prayer that can promote contemplation by accessing the preternatural calling for the sacred presence to cope with times of personal challenge. Moreover, it is essential to the psychology of religion since it is an act of reason that implies the application of the mind to divine things. Praying the Rosary is a supplication that enacts a union between God and humanity, not necessarily to make sense of the ineffable but to petition appropriate gifts and graces from God through praise and thanksgiving.

Coupling psychotherapy research with contemporary neuroscience and traditional methods of seeking grace, such as the Sacred Scripture, prayer, and Bible studies, may provide psycho-spiritual resources that help the faithful cope with personal challenges. Initially, the one body of knowledge, or the Word of the Lord, contained non-academic discursive narratives intended to be understood by ordinary individuals. According to the catechism of the Catholic Church,[22] the current Catholic English Bible includes two main sections: the Old Testament, with forty-six books, and the New Testament, with twenty-seven books. These books include chapters and verses. The Old Testament books are subcategorized as the Pentateuch, Torah or law books, history books, the books of poetry and wisdom, the prophetic books, and the deuterocanonical books. The New Testament contains the four gospels, or the books of Matthew, Mark, Luke, and

---

[22] Catholic Church, *Catechism of the Catholic Church.*

John; the Acts of the Apostles; the Epistles with both the Pauline and the apostolic letters; and the book of Revelation.[23] After World War II, American Christianity witnessed a proliferation of English Bible translations. The 1611 King James Version (KJV, 1769/2017) is the most popular Bible translation in the United States; however, the American Bible Society (2017) reported that most Bible enthusiasts read translations published in the last sixty years. The physically present Bible as the carrier of the Word of the Lord, either opened in the pulpit or in the privacy of the faithful's homes, symbolically engages them in active awareness of God's presence in their daily lives, providing a sense of peace and joy even amid significant life adversities. The faithful use the Bible's teachings to strengthen their relationship with God.

Devout Catholics cited that sacred music can ease anxieties and fears, restore their well-being during personal challenges, and instill prosocial behavior. Musical performance in the liturgy has been a vital component of worship that has shaped the faithful's theological and socioreligious spiritual identity. Contemporary worship combines Biblical spirituality with Christian musicians' artistic authenticity to raise awareness of humankind's trials and tribulations—experiences from sacred music foster cognitive understanding and

---

[23] Libreria Editrice Vaticana, *Catechism of the Catholic Church.*

sensory perception. Sacred music can promote the embodiment of their religious experience beyond their mental convictions.

The Roman Catholic Church instructed her faithful that sins are forgiven by celebrating the sacrament of penance or confession. This ritual is an exchange between the penitent making a brief verbal confession of perceived transgressions and the priest, who acts in *persona Christi* to mediate God's forgiveness and healing by assigning a short penance that may consist of the recitation of familiar prayers such as Our Father and by speaking a formula of absolution. This ritual interchange between the priest's absolution and the penitent's contrition objectively removes the guilt the latter experienced out of sin.

The Christian custom of offering and burning candles in the sanctuary and before statues of saints symbolizes reverence for the flame of sacrifice, love, and the divine presence. The Bible offers a myriad of examples portraying the symbolism of candles, lamps, and lanterns and their light as positive images representing God's presence and blessing,[24] guidance,[25] responsibility,[26] illumination,[27] and life.[28] The use of candles in the devout Catholics' prayers is not necessarily soteriological or concerned with the salvation of the soul itself, but to employ the flame to help in mediation as they entrust their supplications to different intercessors such as saints, the Virgin, or the Lord Jesus Christ, thus creating a solid connection between the devout and the divinity. Furthermore, the wick melting the wax, allowing the flame to exist, symbolizes the flesh and the spirit entrusted to the sacred to petition for help, protection, or blessings in times of adversity. Therefore, candle flames facilitate the faithful's spiritual connection with the divine.

---

[24] Sam. 3:3 KJV.

[25] Prov. 6:23 KJV.

[26] Matt. 25:1–13 KJV.

[27] Luke 15:8 KJV.

[28] Job 29:2–3 KJV.

Summary of Religious Symbols

Various scientific perspectives, such as anthropology, psychology, sociology, and theology, have explored religious symbols and rituals. The mysterious, transcendent, and ineffable symbolism of religious icons, rituals, and sacred sites adds a sense of unity and coherence to sensory experiences that create a particular social connection between individuals remarkably faithful to Catholicism and other religions and beliefs. Sacramentals or sacred objects such as the Bible, the Rosary, crucifixes, iconography, vigil candles, sacred bells, sacred music, incense, holy water, oil anointment, and the church as a site for worship, among other artifacts, facilitate interactions with the divine, creating a trance sensation that encourages a harmonious inner balance state. Religious rites and traditions, such as the sacraments of Eucharist and confession, are associated with intangible aspects of multisensory rituals consisting of distinctive phenomena that are incomprehensible by reasoning while still creating a serene union between God and the devout. Our research showed improved mood, subjective well-being, and life satisfaction when religious individuals were exposed to the multisensory experience of religious symbols and rites. The interaction of human sensoria with the symbolic nature of the sacraments and sacramentals provides the faithful with glimpses of the divine, and this process, together with religious teachings, helps them cope in times of personal challenges.

Religious Teachings

Our research found the importance of religious teaching, which underscored the need to raise awareness and the importance of influential spiritual teachings that encourage effective communication between the faithful by focusing on the relevance of their belief system, religious interpretations, and application to their daily lives. The Catholic Church stresses the significance of respecting the fidelity of God's Word and the faithful's needs when conducting catechetical activity. Religious teachings can occur on Sunday Mass Liturgy, attending the priest's homily, during church communal gatherings of small prayer groups, or learning via spiritual readings in the privacy of the devout's time. The faithful employ various cognitive mechanisms during religious teachings while listening to the priest's sermons, partaking in Bible study assemblies, and engaging in private spiritual readings that may significantly impact their daily lives, foster their mental development, and help them cope with personal challenges. The tradition of the Roman Catholic Church invites the faithful to listen to the ordained minister explain the scriptures proclaimed in the liturgy during Mass and accept the preaching as the Word of God. The purpose of the Christocentric character of the homily is to communicate religious and moral content proclaiming the truth of God to the faithful, helping the faithful to integrate Christ's dying and rising with their personal trials and triumphs, and ultimately becoming in assembly the body of Christ and measuring whether and how devout Catholics listened to sermons from a theological and/or psychological standpoint.

Bible study is crucial for many congregations since it offers the faithful a communal gathering of small prayer groups. In the 1980s, many Catholic churches started building their community by organizing small gatherings to help the faithful grow in their faith. The size of these meetings fosters greater personal intimacy, provides additional opportunities for teaching and instruction in faith, and contributes to higher levels of involvement. In addition, in the small-scale assembly of the faithful, congregation members can connect better, creating a sense of family and infusing relational skills transferable to other social interactions.

The Catholic Church owns powerful mass and digital media systems such as news reports, blogs, forums, and websites, as well as local diocesan magazines, parochial bulletins, local newspapers, the Vatican daily newspaper *L'Osservatore Romano*, the Episcopal Conference daily newspaper, the broadcasting satellite network Tv2000, local TV channels, and bookstores all over the world. The Catholic Church has welcomed digital and mass media venues as a new forum for the gospel that helps disseminate the Word of the Lord together with more traditional delivery methods of religious readings, fostering further interactions with the public and encouraging deep learning based on the understanding, integration, and application of the spiritual readings in their various formats. The Sacred Scripture is the inspiration and content of catechism; however, it is a collection of writings rather than a single, unified publication. Therefore, interpreting its sacred richness requires the reader to carefully analyze the scriptures' historical, literary, and linguistic contexts. Furthermore, the ability to communicate, reflect, discern, and act in an informed and sensitive manner toward the sociocultural expressions of religious traditions corresponds to individuals' level of religious literacy. The church encourages the faithful to cultivate spiritual self-development by nourishing Christian reading based on self-discipline for self-education and fostering the spirit of service.

Summary of Religious Teachings

An increasing body of literature has devoted decades to exploring the effects of religious teachings on issues surrounding individuals' health, well-being, and social cohesion. Various fields of knowledge have indicated greater longevity, decreased mental and physical deterioration, and better ways to cope with personal challenges for those devout individuals who regularly participate in symbolic religious rituals and religious teachings. Our research found that the faithful's religious symbols and religious teachings are biologically significant experiences that incorporate embodied actions, encouraging the allegorical interpretation of an experience that may transform the worshippers' self-perception, increase their self-efficacy, and foster a sense of security, order, and belonging. Comparably, the emotional and cultural components associated with sacred religious symbols and religious teachings allow the faithful to transcend time, space, and self-perceived shortcomings within a symbolic environment. Therefore, using religious symbols, rituals, and teachings creates an extended, alternative reality that facilitates meaningful actions that could serve as a resource to cope with personal challenges.

Cognition and Instruction through Religious Practice and Teaching

Our research explored how religious practices and teachings impact individuals' cognitive structure, soothing their fears and anxieties, forging social bonds, increasing faith, and positively influencing the faithful's spiritual life. The last three decades have shown a growing interest in the cognitive, evolutionary, and behavioral sciences to explore how religiosity originated due to humans' cognitive mechanisms that evolved to solve adaptive problems in ancestral times. Therefore, these constitute a necessary stage in the evolution of the dynamic character of knowledge, occurring when the body interacts with the environment and resulting in adaptation to the social environment. Religion emerged as a cognitive byproduct of the mind; therefore, more intuitive mental individuals tend to be more religious than analytic cognitive ones. Furthermore, religious rituals and symbols leverage social learning that fosters human groups' unification, cooperativeness, and social coherence. Thus, spiritual symbolic practices and teachings generate a sense of stability, predictability, and confidence in the structure of the world, canceling fears of cognitive origin in times of personal challenges and hence improving individuals' overall health. However, religious beliefs are cognitively different beliefs. They constitute social identity markers because they are challenging to verify and may even be empirically untestable, thus forging the faithful's cognitive schemata with a strong influence on their psychology. Therefore, religiosity as a cross-cultural phenomenon is highly complex, affecting the cognitive and behavioral aspects of the human mind.

Religious practice and teachings depend on cognitive representations of norms and roles, not necessarily based on immediate empirical facts or physical realities. When scientific knowledge is not enough to profile the meaning of existence, religious beliefs, with their symbolic practice and teachings, may participate pragmatically in knowledge acquisition via the sacred mysteries, also referred to as the unknown. Therefore, religion is a metadiscourse with a cognitive role. Religiosity refers to specific manifestations of transcendence in concrete social forms, associated with a religious community, symbolic spiritual practices, and religious teachings that provide the faithful with a sense of social and religious identity. Religious practice and teachings provide a sense of meaning and purpose in times of personal challenges, offering psychological integration by promoting a positive and hopeful worldview and embracing cognitive reappraisal of the current circumstances. Religiosity also presents role models within the sacred writings, giving indirect control over adverse events and providing a sense of belonging, thus reducing isolation and loneliness. Therefore, life satisfaction, a measure of the individual's cognitive well-being, is positively associated with religious practices and teachings.

Humans are intrinsically symbolic. Numeric, linguistic, or religious symbols regulate their cognition and behavior. Extant research suggests that symbols evolved from motivated and nonarbitrary signs, meaning associations, or iconic signs, resembling their meanings. However, regarding the symbolic nature of religiosity, the faithful's cognitive style affects how they process the religious contents. An extended cognitive approach makes the authentic embrace, thinking about the meaning of their beliefs with an analytic mind. They may be more open to alternative interpretations, thus accepting any ambiguities or the hidden meaning of a given story with greater tolerance. However, a more literal cognitive style needs cognitive closure, seeking fixed answers with a closed view. Nonetheless, extant research indicates that religious practices and teachings firmly integrated into individuals' worldviews provide meaning, providing perspective that may mitigate the effects of cognitive dissonance by reducing the discrepancies between the faithful's beliefs and their life circumstances. Overall, even when beliefs and experiences may not always align with individuals, religious practices and teachings may help them cope better during personal challenges, providing a powerful source of comfort.

Religious, symbolic rituals are highly intricate manifestations of human behavior. They preserve social order, promote a sense of community belonging, and incorporate embodied action. Therefore, understanding the effects of religious symbols, rituals, and teachings on the faithful's cognitive lives is a powerful cultural tool for exploring collective symbolic coping. The broad implications of the epistemic and pragmatic functions of cognitive dissonance inherent to religious teaching and learning have been widely documented. Being alert to mental inconsistencies allows individuals to learn and change their course of action. Devout Catholics find the pedagogical tools to guide their transformation by learning about the sacraments. Catholic education aims to transmit the Catholic faith, promoting and contributing to society's spiritual and secular well-being by fostering tolerance, respect, and inclusivity. Catholic teachings aim to develop human faculties, such as proper judgment and a sense of values, such as justice, humility, simplicity, love of God, and goodness, to help them cope with personal challenges. Furthermore, religious education prepares individuals to serve the community, building the individuals' character and competence. Thus, spiritual teachings help individuals become agents of transformation within their inner circle, the church, and society.

Extant research abounds on empirical evidence of the benefits of religious practices and teachings for the mental health of individuals. Furthermore, the scientific study of the psychology of religion benefits individuals since it provides them with the necessary knowledge about their religious behaviors and mental processes. Additionally, spiritual teachings help individuals focus better on previously ambiguous or unknown dimensions of religious phenomena. Finally, the communal aspect of learning about religious practices is associated with a lower risk of all-cause mortality, subsequent health, and better life satisfaction. The *Catechism of the Catholic Church*[29] teaches the dogma that concerns specifically what the church believes was revealed by God, making some teachings explicit that were previously implicit in divine revelation and adding dimensions to the faithful's perception of the symbolic nature of their religious beliefs. A doctrine is the teachings of the church or anything the church proposes for belief beyond scripture and distinct from the revelation of God by communicating truth to man beyond the ordinary course of action. Religious teachings are also instrumental in promoting interfaith dialogue that helps comprehend the diversity of belief systems. The natural capacity of the human intellect to get knowledge and expand can be elevated to the next level when individuals learn about the three theological virtues of faith, will, and charity through language, symbols, sacramental rites, and the Liturgy. Furthermore, Catholic education can promote a sense of the Catholic community, which is essential for a critical perspective that views learning as a process of development, transformation, and humanization.

Catholic teachings aim for intellectual growth and alignment with spiritual, emotional, social, and religious expansion. Therefore, the teaching resources must stem from a standpoint that includes morality, talent, and enthusiasm. Catechism relies on storytelling as a powerful tool for transformation because it illuminates profound truths, passes on history, and builds bridges between faith and cul-

---

[29] Libreria Editrice Vaticana, Catechism of the Catholic Church.

tural traditions. Furthermore, the ministry of Catholic teaching or catechism promulgates growth in the faithful's hearts, instilling a sense of spiritual trust, sparking a change in their minds, and infusing the importance of knowing, believing, and improving their doing while strengthening their will. Also, the cognitive and emotional representations that underlie sacred and inviolable beliefs and symbolic religious practices and teachings affect the individuals' social and personal behaviors, modulating the sensory perceptions that help them cope in times of unique challenges and providing them with a sense of comfort and contentment. The current literature review provided the foundational conceptualization and integrative efforts that clarified, broadened, and informed the present study, which sought to understand how devout Catholics described how they used religious symbols and religious teachings to cope with personal challenges.

Our research focused on the relationship between religious symbols, moral decision-making, and individual religious beliefs. Based on historical context and our findings, religious imagery promoted individuals' thoughts and behaviors that encouraged social cohesion, more effective coping in times of adversity, and greater life satisfaction. We found that religious identity commitment positively predicted individuals' self-perceived well-being. The social context, as a body of knowledge, behaviors, rites, and values, promotes interfaith dialogue to understand the diversity of beliefs in different cultures. We also explored the neuro-physiological effects of the correlation between religious coping and psychological stress. Anecdotal evidence suggests that increasing knowledge of the neuro-biological factors associated with religiosity is a workable strategy to cope with adversity.

Findings of Impacts Of Religiosity: Transformative Power of Symbolism and Spirituality through the Lens of Neuroscience And Psychology

As we have seen over the last few decades, many studies have found indisputable evidence of how our religious beliefs, rituals, symbolism, and teachings significantly impact the devout's cognitive and behavioral functions. Also, within the last five years, much research has identified the effects of religiosity or spirituality on the individual's physical, neurobiological, and psychological aspects. These findings constitute an emerging research trend in religious sociology. Because one of us was born and raised within a Catholic environment, we decided to conduct our research study with devout Catholics in the United States of America, specifically in southeastern Virginia, where one of us resides, who used religious symbols and religious teachings regularly and actively worshipped in a church building or remotely a minimum of once a month. We preselected the most traditional and widely known Catholic religious symbols and teachings that the devout would most certainly resort to to help them cope in times of adversity. We achieved a final sample of thirty-six participants who answered the preinterview questionnaire, of which twenty-five individuals participated in the interviews.

Of the thirty-six participants who completed the questionnaire, twenty-five were older than fifty-one, and twenty-nine had been devout Catholics for over twenty-one years. Thirty-two of the participants were white or Caucasian, and four were Hispanic. Therefore, the results show a lack of representation of other ethnicities and younger adults in this research study, which may be the subject of future research. We were interested in exploring the frequency and relevance of using religious symbols and teachings to help individuals cope in times of personal challenges. Figure 1 shows a count for each religious symbol and the teaching the participants found most helpful. We can see that 44 percent of the participants attributed the Rosary as the most helpful symbol among the thirteen religious symbols and three religious teachings. Similarly, 44 percent attributed religious readings as the most helpful religious teaching in times of personal challenges. However, only three or fewer participants selected the oil anointment, church bells, or holy water to help them cope with adversity.

Figure 1

Count of Religious Symbols and Religious Teachings Found Most Helpful in Times of Personal Challenges

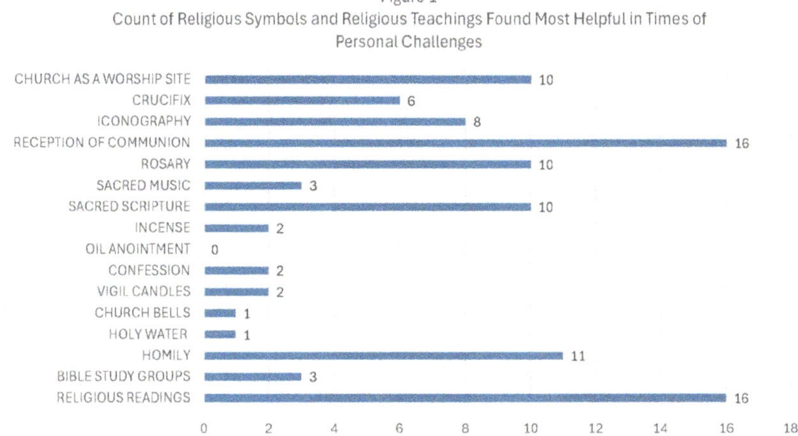

Four main trends emerged from the data analysis. The first one was related to how the use of religious symbols and teachings made the individuals feel the presence of God. The second trend accounted for how using religious symbols and teachings helped individuals find solace during adversity. The third trend gave thorough insights into understanding social interactions by attributing, negotiating, and interpreting the meaning of religious symbols and teachings. The fourth trend demonstrated the feelings of faith that emerged from using religious symbols and teachings during adversity.

Each trend reflected individuals' sense of intimate connection with Divinity that helped them cope, especially during the most challenging times of their lives. The responses that shared the sense of not being alone and feeling loved and worth it, despite their difficult circumstances, were overwhelming. They walked in faith, not in sight. Furthermore, when the individuals talked about their adversities, these included all types of problems or issues that affected them internally, such as physical, mental, or emotional health-related matters, or externally, such as financial struggles. Their challenges ranged from stressful situations to the most profound tragedies, such as the suicide of siblings and offspring, fighting cancer, addictions, and associations with the wrong crowds.

Additionally, we found that people attribute meaning to the symbols and teachings. They negotiate with others their interpretation in the quest to obtain a sense of belonging, understanding, and togetherness within their communities, which helps them cope with adversity more effectively than when they face challenges in isolation. Based on symbolic interactionism theory (SIT), our theoretical foundation emphasizes that shared symbols give us a sense of unity and help establish the coherence of our sensory experiences. Also, we negotiate reality through symbol interpretation, which involves complex mental processes.

Finally, the feelings that emerged from religious symbols and teachings encompassed recentering, a higher perspective, a sense of otherworldly protection, joy, and spiritual nourishment. The impact of religiosity on the physical, neurobiological, and psychological aspects of believers' lives has captured the interest of scientists for the last five years. There is a growing trend to trace the effects of religious practices, beliefs, and teachings on people's cognition, behavior, and emotions. Many empirical studies have explored how we can alleviate our mental discomfort from conflicting beliefs, attitudes, or values simply by using religious teachings, rituals, or symbols. Various researchers have investigated how religiosity or spiritual practices can help us soothe fears and anxieties, forge prosocial behavior, improve mental development, and enhance the quality of our daily lives.

The tenets of SIT framed our research. The American philosopher, sociologist, and psychologist George Herbert Mead (1863–1931) was SIT's founding father, who theorized about the unique ability of individuals to employ language and symbols to communicate. We based our research on a theory that expounded on the sense of unity and coherence of sensory experiences and the symbolization processing and interaction through shared symbols established among individuals. We further believe that the functions individuals attached to a particular object, image, or symbol made it meaningful based on what they thought and perceived rather than what was objectively true. Even when there is a growing interest in learning more about how religiosity and spirituality are associated with overall well-being and life satisfaction, there was not much research on how the devout from a specific religion, in this case, Catholics, described the use of religious symbols and religious teachings to help them cope in times of personal challenges.

After one-on-one interviews with the participants, we concluded that sacramentals or sacred objects such as the Bible, the Rosary, crucifixes, iconography, or religious music, among others, facilitated an inner connection with the divine, creating a trance-like feeling that encouraged a harmonious internal balance state. However, our descriptive data showed that some religious symbols and teachings were more significant than others in helping the participants cope with adversity. For example, the Rosary and spiritual readings were described as very helpful by 44 percent of the questionnaire participants in assisting them in times of personal challenges. On the contrary, few participants described using Bible study groups or oil anointment to help them cope with adversity.

Regarding the frequency of religious symbols and teachings, the results varied depending on the accessibility of each ritual, practice, or teaching. For example, the crucifix was readily available to the participants; therefore, it was the most widely used symbol to help them cope during difficult times. However, the reception of Communion or the oil anointment can only be sacredly accessed with the aid of the clergy administering during specific times. Finally, Bible study groups were another religious teaching that was not frequently used to help people cope during times of adversity. The reason Bible study groups are not used frequently is a weak consensus on how Bible study groups benefit individuals in understanding the Word of the Lord better or coping with personal challenges.

Four main trends emerged from the data analysis. The first trend was related to how the use of religious symbols and teachings made individuals feel the presence of God. The overwhelming response of the participants showed undisputed intimate moments with God when they were performing religious rituals and using symbols and teachings that made them feel cared for, loved, and relieved from their burdens. The findings suggested an overall sense of feeling closer to the sphere of God's presence as they described how the sensory aspect of symbols transported their spirit. Additionally, the participants described how using religious symbols and teachings reminded them that God was asking them to trust and have more faith in Him.

The second trend accounted for how using religious symbols and teachings helped individuals find solace during adversity. Many studies link religiosity with a sense of well-being and life satisfaction that helps the faithful cope better with personal challenges. We were interested in exploring how individuals coped better with stressful situations, tragedy, and mental, emotional, and physiological issues with religious symbols and teachings. Our participants described various moments of personal challenges that required mental strength and concentration, such as going on a combat mission, sleepless nights due to anxiety, or completing a graduate degree. Other individuals described adversities that involved tragedies such as suicide in the family, strokes, and untimely death due to accidents. Even others described mental and emotional difficulties, such as attempted suicide, fighting different types of addictions, affiliations with the wrong crowd, or being laid off. Finally, other individuals talked about personal challenges that involved physiological issues such as surgeries, different types of cancer, and various life-threatening diseases. These findings were significant in depth and intensity. For example, some participants described how praying the Rosary helped them find solace by giving them peace and a connection to a lifeline or lifeboat. Others said humming or listening to sacred music empowered them when their strengths were depleted.

The third trend provided thorough insights into understanding social interactions by attributing, negotiating, and interpreting the meaning of religious symbols and teachings. This specific trend identified and supported the tenets of our theoretical foundation, symbolic interactionism theory (SIT). This study explored the participants' narratives in depth, highlighting how they assigned meanings to a particular object, image, or symbol based on what they believed and perceived rather than what was objectively true and providing a sense of unity and belonging when interacting with others through shared symbols. For example, one participant ascribed the reception of Communion to the meaning of being the source and summit of his life. Others attributed to the holy water the definitions of a sign of birth and death, finiteness, and infinity.

Regarding social interactions, the findings showed that individuals negotiated reality by employing complex cognitive processes that combined social information with their meaning when using shared symbols and lived experiences. For example, some participants described how receiving Communion with their families and church community gave them a sense of peace and comfort while connecting with others through shared religious practices. Others described how religious teachings, such as Bible study groups, were helpful because they provided them with a cohort of people with shared values to be among during times of challenge.

Concerning the participants' interpretation based on their use of religious symbols and teachings, this study's findings showed, for example, that people interpreted church bells as a calling to Mass, like a timer or clock. Even others described their interpretation of receiving Communion as the reception of the real presence of God on a vertical plane, while receiving Communion with other churchgoers signified the presence of God on a horizontal plane.

The fourth trend demonstrated the feeling of faith that emerged from using religious symbols and teachings during adversity. The participants described feelings of recentering and getting a higher perspective, as well as otherworldly protection, joy, and spiritual nourishment. Based on the findings, religious symbols and teachings helped individuals refocus their minds with humility and empathy, helping them gain peace and more profound insight into the meaning of life. In addition, their narratives demonstrated a sense of empowerment, healing, and cleansing by feeling within the miraculous and fortifying sanctuary that helped them cope when they struggled with their internal turmoil. Furthermore, individuals described feeling uplifted when rejoicing in the beauty and comfort of religious symbols and teachings. The findings demonstrated an overall sense of kindness, trust, faith, and hope that emerged with the use of religious symbols and religious teachings. Furthermore, others described feelings of humility, empathy, inner peace, miraculous coincidences, protection, and comfort in times of adversity.

The individuals' reactions were awe-inspiring when they described their feelings of otherworldly protection. For example, one participant felt protected when praying for the Rosary while flying into combat. Others said that using religious symbols during challenging times made them sense miraculous occurrences since these events were statistically close to impossible to be coincidences. Even others described listening to the sound of church bells and smelling incense as a way to witness God's power to rejoice despite their personal challenges.

With this book, the first in our spiritual well-being series, we intend to provide new insights that could help solve significant problems when applied in professional practices. Furthermore, religious educators, such as catechists, clinicians with religious backgrounds, counselors, and researchers, may benefit from an in-depth understanding of how using religious symbols and teachings can help the devout cope with adversity. Moreover, the content of this book, derived from a research study, has the potential to be of great assistance to clergy members, chaplains, health-care providers, and researchers in enhancing their person-centered approach. This approach will involve integrating individuals' religious backgrounds into health-care assessments, treatments, and interventions. Especially during times of stress and tragedy and when dealing with mental, emotional, and physiological challenges, deepening our comprehension of how to improve coping strategies warrants the scientific community's time, financial support, and collaborative efforts. Consequently, further research in this area will contribute to the community's understanding of how individuals attribute, interpret, and navigate the significance of shared symbols and teachings to enhance their coping abilities.

The emerging field of neurotheology, or spiritual neuroscience, portends that the brain responds in specific ways to contemplative healing practices, producing emotions and promoting metaphorical healing (Gaitán and Castresana 2021; Klemm 2022; Papantoniou and Vionis 2020). Therefore, our message in this book may trigger future researchers to explore how symbology and religious, or spiritual, teachings may facilitate the devout's coping mechanisms in times of adversity. In our series, we will delve next into the developing AI era and its implications for spirituality, religiosity, and coping in times of adversity. We will explore how artificial intelligence and machine learning influence the devout's beliefs and interpretations and thus respond to findings about the benefits of spiritual practices as another way to cope when facing life's inevitable challenges. Similarly, we will explore, in the series to come, how the devout from different religious affiliations describe how their symbols and teachings help them cope in times of personal challenges. We invite you to consider how spiritual symbology and teachings may be included in future discussions with diverse populations, such as business or academic communities, to promote an evidence-based overall sense of well-being, especially in times of adversity. Most importantly, we are passionate about exploring the overlooked role of spirituality or religiosity in mental health and psychological well-being to provide further resources to help individuals cope with life's adversities. Furthermore, we will explore the psycho-social role of ritualized communication in individuals' mental and emotional health to promote inner peace, build community, create a sense of belonging, and strengthen trust and hope.

Conclusion

Religious symbols, teachings, and practices play a significant role in individuals' lives, impacting their mental, emotional, and social well-being. These were the fundamental findings from our research with devout Catholics over a year ago. These elements provide meaning, comfort, and social connection, especially during challenging times. Previous research and our findings showed that religious practices can ease anxieties, build social bonds, and even influence how individuals perceive the world. Although our study focused on devout Catholics and their use of religious symbols and teachings, the findings highlight the broader importance of these aspects in various spiritual and religious practices. Through shared symbols and interpretations, individuals find a sense of belonging, help them to navigate complex emotions, and construct meaning.

Religion and spirituality shape our worldview, influencing how we make sense of ourselves, the world, and our place within it. Our findings taught us that religion and spirituality create optimistic perspectives, fostering social connection and reducing isolation. By turning inward through faith, we become more aware of our physical sensations and emotions, amplifying the usually subtle aspects of our being. Spirituality, or faith-heightened awareness, deepens our spiritual experience, making it feel more natural and tangible and strengthening our faith and belief. Religious symbols are crucial in this process, influencing our emotions and offering comfort during hardships. Research highlights the importance of religious education incorporating social and cultural elements, as these contexts further shape individuals' understanding of their faith and the world. The need to further explore how religious symbols and teachings help us overcome difficulties was the reason for our curiosity and the force that took us on a journey to complete a series about this topic.

From the perspective of devout Catholics, their faith plays a significant role in enhancing their lives. Religious practices shape individual and community worldviews, strengthening the connection to God and interpreting scripture. These practices establish norms that guide and provide stability. Although not all Catholics participate equally (with varying levels of Mass attendance, prayer, and adherence to tradition), they find meaning and strength through their faith. Catholic identity is deeply rooted in liturgical reverence and principles like *opus Dei* (God's work) and *lex orandi* (prayer). These principles emphasize adhering to traditions and practices to preserve Catholicism and activate individuals' spirituality. To this point, we found positive correlations between religious practices and self-efficacy, demonstrating how faith can empower individuals to overcome challenges.

However, modernizing society and busy lifestyles have led to declining participation in some spiritual practices. This has led to the rise of different types of Catholics, categorized as creative (adhere to some aspects), orthodox (fully endorse traditions), and cultural (occasionally practice rituals without strong belief), reflecting the evolving nature of the faith in a secular era. Our study aims to raise awareness of the importance of effective religious communication in supporting individuals' belief systems, fostering spiritual interpretation, and promoting public understanding of religion. By exploring prominent symbols and teachings, the research seeks to understand what remains relevant in this changing landscape.

Devout Catholics have a rich tradition of using religious symbols, rituals, and teachings to navigate the challenges of everyday life, such as seeking better health and resilience during hardships. Devout Catholics believe the power of religious symbols lies in their ability to transcend individual differences and unite people across cultures. These symbols, interpreted through various cognitive and emotional lenses, act as building blocks for rituals. Rituals provide a sense of order, community engagement, and personal transformation. They often involve repetitive actions, sounds, and sights that stimulate the senses and leave lasting impressions. For instance, ringing church bells evokes joy, connection, and God's presence.

Similarly, the crucifix serves as a reminder of Christ's sacrifice and offers comfort during personal struggles. Beyond symbols like the Rosary, religious teachings like the Holy Scriptures also contribute to coping mechanisms. The Bible serves as a source of guidance. It strengthens the relationship with God, while the Rosary fosters contemplation and intercessory prayer. Our study focused on thirteen common Catholic symbols and three specific teachings, exploring their historical context and uses. Our findings highlighted the multisensory nature of faith and how various elements, including soundscapes, sacred music, and incense, contribute to the overall well-being of devout individuals.

We also focused on the Catholic perspective, highlighting how their teachings aim for intellectual and emotional growth while fostering social well-being and interfaith dialogue. We found a complex interplay between religious beliefs, cognitive processes, and personal well-being. We discovered the potential of spiritual practices for coping with adversity across diverse populations and faiths. The findings contribute to the growing body of research on the impact of religiosity and spirituality on mental and emotional well-being. Our discovery advocates integrating individuals' religious backgrounds into health-care assessments and interventions to enhance person-centered care. We also believe incorporating religious symbols and teachings into mental health interventions could benefit everyday practice. We can create more comprehensive and inclusive support systems by acknowledging the diverse ways individuals find meaning and cope with adversity. We derived the following four objectives:

- *Mental and emotional benefits:* Religious involvement soothes anxieties, strengthens social bonds, and improves life satisfaction. This positive influence comes from a sense of meaning, purpose, and belonging, as well as hope and optimism fostered by religious beliefs.

- *Cognitive frameworks:* Religious symbols, rituals, and teachings provide a lens through which individuals understand and navigate the world. They create a sense of structure, predictability, and comfort, reducing anxieties and facilitating cognitive reappraisal during challenges.
- *Coping mechanisms:* By explaining challenging situations and providing role models, religious practices equip individuals with tools to overcome personal difficulties, such as reducing cognitive dissonance and the discomfort caused by conflicting beliefs and experiences.
- *Community and identity:* Religious practices and teachings act as markers of social identity and foster a sense of belonging within a community. This shared experience and knowledge supports individuals and lessens feelings of isolation.

This research opens the door for further exploration in the field of religious sociology and its connection to individual well-being. By delving deeper into diverse perspectives and fostering interfaith understanding, we can gain valuable insights into how individuals navigate adversity and find meaning in their lives. No doubt, we are social beings in search of meaning. When we incorporate both elements into our lives in alignment with our values and principles, we enhance our sense of well-being and satisfaction. According to a 2023 report from the National Survey Data, 7 in 10 US adults describe themselves as spiritual in some way. Eighty-three percent (83%) believe people have a soul beyond their physical body. Seventy-four percent (74%) believe that there are things that science cannot possibly explain. There is still much for us to uncover between the inner human perspective and understanding and making a connection to religiosity and spirituality. We are also lucky or unlucky depending on the individual interpretation that we are living in a technological breakthrough in our lifetime. It may appear far-fetched why artificial intelligence (AI) and machine learning have anything to do with religiosity and spirituality. But they do.

How do AI and religiosity mingle? What do they have in common? We all drift and daydream; we trust our gut and are often baffled by our actions. Our memories may absorb all sorts of irrelevant data and neglect the most crucial details of an experience. Could machines reproduce the messiness of our minds? Language models "hallucinate," causing errors induced by incorrect assumptions made by the model, biases in the data used to train the model, or insufficient training data. Doesn't it sound familiar?

Now bear with us for a moment as we develop these concepts. Considering that the Age of Enlightenment, the intellectual movement of the late seventeenth century and the eighteenth century, emphasized reason, individualism, and skepticism, we could argue that symbolic logic, born by George Boole (1815–1864), the founder of pure mathematics and computer science, was rooted in the Enlightenment notion that humans are ruled by reason. If that is the case, then symbolic logic and studying symbolic abstractions that capture the formal features of logical inference by using basic symbols to remove the ambiguity that comes with using language could be at the root of deep learning—the method that enables AI to teach computers to process data in a way that is inspired by the human brain.

Now let us go even more profoundly and link AI's functioning with modern psychology's insights regarding associatory and latent motivations that often drive our behaviors. It could be claimed that psychoanalysis regards the subconscious as a "psychological automatism," similar to what we call a machine. Lacan[30] believed the subconscious was constituted by an algorithmic or binary language, just like computer code. Even Carl Jung's (1875–1961) view of the psyche could be associated with the principles behind generative AI. The Swiss psychiatrist, the founder of analytical psychology, believed that we all shared four essential functions—sensation, intuition, thinking, and feeling. These were part of the collective unconscious, encompassing the patterns and reactions of the mind shared by people worldwide. Therefore, he envisioned the human race starting with

---

[30] Burnham, "Lacan."

a dormant knowledge of shared symbols rather than coming with a "blank slate" or "tabula rasa." This collective concept of the subconscious could draw similarities with how the advanced AI models are built by compiling mammoth amounts of data that contain a vast percentage of our cultural past and current developments. That being said, at the current level of development, the models still refuse to talk about controversial topics, and caveats and disclaimers often restrain their authority. The chatbots still do not possess intrinsic agency or desires. The chatbots (AI runs) are programmed to learn to predict and reflect the user's preferences. They also lack embodied experience in the world, including first-person memories. However, could it be that AI is pure subconscious, without a genuine ego hiding behind their personas? How about AI and, in this case, Catholics?

There is a new Catholic program that uses AI, Magisterium AI. It is promising to revolutionize academic research in Catholic education. It can potentially disrupt long-held doctrines and beliefs, providing users with information on Catholic doctrine, teachings, and canon law. This AI program, though, is carefully curated. It can be used by priests seeking to write a homily, canon lawyers looking for the latest updates, and researchers wishing to access Catholic documents from the ancient past. Even the pope is incorporating discussions on AI to promote dialogue and ethical reflection on its use.

Another topic of interest relates to Google's artificial intelligence system, Language Model for Dialogue Applications (LaMDA), and the possibility of developing a level of sentience similar to that of a person. Google disagrees and cautions against this concept since LaMDA is a system that draws on billions upon billions of words written by human beings to produce responses to questions. Thus, they may feel real, but that is the effect of "anthropomorphizing" such models. From a Catholic perspective, the pope and the Vatican have addressed the topic in recent years. In 2020, Pope Francis invited Catholics worldwide to pray that robotics and artificial intelligence remain permanently at the service of human beings. The Vatican emphasizes transparency, inclusion, accountability, impartiality, reliability, security, and privacy.

So here is a set of questions for you to ponder, my dear readers: Can the faithful accept the transferring the omnipresence/omniscience of God to Google? Or will they resist, seeing this as an incursion into divine territory? Can we conduct experiments using artificial intelligence and machine learning in order to understand religiosity better and, conversely, use religiosity to understand artificial intelligence better? So what is AI? Is it what is portrayed in Hal in *2001, A Space Odyssey, The Terminator*, or *The Matrix* movies, or even in the series *Humans* and HBO's *Westworld*? In our next series, we will explore the dangers of putting AI on a deity pedestal because its level of intelligence goes beyond most humans and appears limitless. It can be creative beyond our wildest imagination. It does not have to pay bills, does not age, and does not have hormonal turmoil, physical pain, hunger, or sexual desire. It is immortal. Wow! That got your attention…didn't it? Let's meet in our next series. You will be fascinated by our findings!

References

American Bible Society. 2017. Accessed February, 2024. https:// bibleresources.americanbible.org/resource/a-brief-description-of-popular-bible-translations.

Burnham, Clint. "Lacan and the Algorithm." *CLCWeb: Comparative Literature and Culture* 24.4 (2022). Accessed March 2, 2024. https://doi.org/10.7771/1481-4374.4116.

Carlson, S. J., Levine, L. J., Lench, H. C., Flynn, E., Carpenter, Z. K., Perez, K. A., and S. W. Bench. (2021). You Shall Go Forth with Joy: Religion and Aspirational Judgments about Emotion. *Psychology of Religion and Spirituality*. Accessed February 2, 2024. https://doi.org/10.1037/rel0000327.

Catholic Church. 1997. *Catechism of the Catholic Church.* Second Edition. Washington, DC: United States Catholic Conference. Accessed February 2, 2024.

Center for Applied Research in the Apostolate. 2022. "Frequently Requested Church Statistics." US Data over Time (Data set). Georgetown University. Accessed February 2, 2024. https://cara. georgetown.edu/frequently-requested-church-statistics.

Chappell, C., Tomcho, T., and R. Foels. 2020. "Psychology of Religion Courses in the Undergraduate Curriculum." *Psychology of Religion and Spirituality*, 12(2): 241–246. Accessed February 2, 2024. https://doi.org/10.1037/rel0000188.

Chepkemoi, J. 2019. "US States by Population of Catholics." WorldAtlas. Accessed March 10, 2024. https://www.worldatlas. com/articles/us-states-by-population-of-catholics.html.

Dentale, F., Vecchione, M., Shariff, A., Verrastro, V., Petruccelli, I., Diotaiuti, P., Petruccelli, F., and C. Barbaranelli. 2018. "Only Believers Rely on God? A New Measure to Investigate Catholic Faith Automatic Associations and Their Relationship with Psychological Well-Being." *Psychology of Religion and Spirituality*, 10(2): 185–194. Accessed March 10, 2024. https://doi-org.lopes.idm.oclc.org/10.1037/rel0000141.

Imperatori, C., Bersani, F. S., Massullo, C., Carbone, G. A., Salvati, A., Mazzi, G., Cicerale, G., Carrara, A., and B. Farina. 2020. "Neuro-Physiological Correlates of Religious Coping to Stress: A Preliminary EEG Power Spectra Investigation." *Neuroscience Letters*, 728, 134956. Accessed February, 2024. https://doi.org/10.1016/j.neulet.2020.134956.

Jung, C. G., Von Franz, M. L., Henderson, J. L., Jaffé, A., and J. Jacobi. 1964. *Man and His Symbols*. Vol. 5183. Dell. Accessed March 10, 2024.

Kahl, B. 2018. "Cross and Trophy." *Studia Theologica*, 72(2): 112–131. Accessed February 2, 2024. https://doi-org.lopes.idm.oclc.org/10.1080/0039338X.2018.1527053.

Kovačević, V., Malenica, K., and G. Kardum. 2021. "Symbolic Interactions in Popular Religion according to Dimensions of Religiosity: A Qualitative Study." *Societies*, 11(2): 30. Accessed February 2, 2024. https://doi.org/10.3390/soc11020030.

Libreria Editrice Vaticana. 2019. *Catechism of the Catholic Church*. 2nd Edition. United States Catholic Conference of Bishops. Accessed March 10, 2024.

Mahić, A. 2019. "Two Home Stoups from the Holdings of the Archaeological Museum of Istria." *Histria archaeologica: Časopis Arheološkog muzeja Istre*, 49(49): 137–156. Accessed March 10, 2024.

Plaatjies-van Huffel, M. A. 2020. "Rethinking the Reciprocity between Lex Credendi, Lex Orandi, and Lex Vivendi: As We Believe, So We Worship. As We Believe, So We live." *HTS Teologiese Studies/Theological Studies*, 76(1). Accessed Marh 10, 2024.

Stroope, S., and J. O. Baker. 2018. "Whose Moral Community? Religiosity, Secularity, and Self-Rated Health across Communal Religious Contexts." *Journal of Health and Social Behavior*, 59(2), 185–199. Accessed February 2, 2024. https://doi.org/10.1177/0022146518755698.

About the Authors

Dr. Frankie Lee is from Phoenix, Arizona, US. He is an educator, researcher, innovator, coach, and mentor whose focus is to drive excellence and continuous growth—personally, professionally, and academically. He utterly believes in discovery and lifelong learning. This concept is ingrained in him: you stop living when you stop learning. He earned his PhD in general and environmental psychology, an executive MBA in global growth strategy and management, and a master's in information management. He is multidisciplined and multilingual. In addition to English, he is fluent in three different dialects of Chinese—Mandarin, Cantonese, and Chow Zhou—and he also speaks Vietnamese. His parents and grandparents were stuck in Vietnam during the Vietnam War, so for the first twelve years of his life, he grew up in Vietnam. They were lucky to leave Vietnam for the US in 1989 due to his mother's wit and foresight. They landed in Boston, Massachusetts, where he attended high school and college and worked professionally in the technology and securities industry before he moved to Arizona in 2003. His professional disciplines are computer information systems, finance, business administration and management, architecture, interior design, construction, real estate and investment, general psychology, environmental psychology, academics, research, and higher education.

Professionally, he has led in a leadership capacity in IT, network security, innovation, construction, and operations in various industries, from governmental agencies to technology, financial and securities, health care, and academia. His applied research focuses on human behaviors, mental health and well-being, and the psychological effects of environmental, spatial, spiritual, or other natural or unnatural forces. He has published studies in various journals and publications. He looks forward to continuing to contribute knowledge to society on many fronts.

Dr. Cristina Leira is from Buenos Aires, Argentina. Her rich Italian and Spanish heritage ignited her passion for languages and cultures. As a native Spanish speaker, fluent in English and French, and proficient in Italian and Portuguese, she has embarked on a journey as a teacher of English and French as second and foreign languages. Her academic pursuits led to her attending the University of Buenos Aires, where she honed her linguistic skills and graduated as a public translator and interpreter. She served as the translator for the Argentinean Instruction, Improvement, and Experimentation Center to ensure that all training material for the National Civil Administration and the State Operational Safety Services was correctly connected to the Air Traffic Control Services. She later taught at the elementary and high school levels. Her thirst for knowledge brought her to the university classroom, where she taught translation and interpretation theory and practice in language acquisition.

Her journey led her to the United States, where she pursued a master's in applied linguistics. During this time, she assumed the role of a district court interpreter. She translated various materials spanning commerce, literature, artwork, and government documents. Eventually, she found her calling as the foreign language and culture program manager for one of the largest US Naval Special Warfare Commands within the Department of Defense. She has collaborated closely with US Navy SEALs for over two decades and maintained a *secret* clearance with the US government. In this high-stakes role, she exercised critical thinking and problem-solving skills to navigate complex, volatile environments, fostering connections across diverse cultures with unwavering kindness, respect, and inclusivity. Throughout her career, she immersed herself in the study of symbology, its evolution, interpretation, and profound impact on individuals' well-being, life satisfaction, and mental and emotional health as a coping mechanism during adversity.

Today, she holds a PhD in general psychology in cognition and instruction and a master of arts in applied linguistics, as well as graduate studies in translation and interpretation. She is a certified neurobiological, ontological, and neurolinguistic coach specializing in mindset transformation, communication techniques, curriculum development, and cultural awareness and integration. Her academic journey led to research in neuroscience and the intricacies of spirituality. Her innovative research illuminates how symbolic interactionism empowers individuals to navigate personal challenges with resilience and grace. She is dedicated to raising awareness, facilitating growth, and guiding individuals on their journey to higher levels of life satisfaction, even in the face of adversity. Her extensive career and academic achievements underscore her unwavering commitment to bridging linguistic and cultural gaps, promoting well-being, and nurturing the human spirit. She is passionate about empowering individuals to thrive and find fulfillment in their unique life paths.

www.ingramcontent.com/pod-product-compliance
Lightning Source LLC
Chambersburg PA
CBHW040743120726
48007CB00007B/79